Breathing *with* God

A Journey into the Magnificent

Stacy Isabelle

ISBN: 0615492843
ISBN-13: 9780615492841

Cover illustration by Donella Vitale.

For
The Beautiful One

CONTENTS

1   Think Beauty   1

2   Be Beauty   69

3   See Beauty   83

4   Thanks To   125

"When love fills your life, all limitations are gone."
—*The Peace Pilgrim*

Every time someone reads a page from this book, I believe God feels a kiss on the cheek. It is my burning desire that the Benevolent One feels millions, and millions, and a million more kisses.
—*Stacy Isabelle*

THINK BEAUTY

INTRODUCTION

I often wonder what it would be like to eavesdrop on the mind of God and witness, first-hand, who we are in Truth. I imagine all our fears, worries, self-doubts and perceived troubles would dissipate in a brilliant flash, making room for only love, appreciation and gratitude, if we really understood how deeply we are loved.

Here are a few thoughts I envision the Benevolent One thinking.

*You are the absolute love of My life. No good thing could I,
or would I, withhold from you.*

—God

In all ways, you are beautiful.

—God

Your mortal mind cannot comprehend
the enormous love and acceptance I have for you,
but ask Me to show you anyway.

—God

You can never outrun My gentle embrace.

—God

Yes, I will stay and comfort you. It is impossible for Me to do anything else.

—God

Your perfect sacredness is all I can see.

—God

You resemble Me in every way, although you often try to deny it.

—God

All darkness eventually bows to My Light.

—God

You matter.
You matter absolutely to Me.

—God

I couldn't possibly be any closer.

—God

You are free. Release yourself.

—God

Breathe. Accept. Love.

—God

It is possible. Hold steadfast to your dreams.
Together we cannot fail.

—God

Yes, of course I will help you.

—God

Relax. I am here. Trust Me.

—God

You need not suffer. Welcome Me, instead of pain.

—God

When you are tempted to feel discouraged, simply look at Me.

—God

All of heaven delights in your happiness.

—God

I could never abandon you. I love you.

—God

Reach for My hand and you will understand,
you are never alone.

—God

INTRODUCTION

One morning, while visualizing a big dream I wanted to fulfill, fear began to settle in and I became doubtful. I started questioning whether I had what it took to accomplish something big and beautiful. I was having difficulty seeing myself as a success in this particular area. So I did what I always do, when self-doubt squeaks into my mind. I asked God for a miracle, a new way of seeing my life and this situation. I asked to see the circumstances with the eyes of Truth, not fear. Then I released everything.

On my drive into work that morning, a digital message in front of a church caught my attention. The message read, "P.U.S.H.—Pray Until Something Happens." That simple statement was the reassurance I needed. It showed me how to see beyond my ego related fears, by staying in prayer. I realized, in that moment, I needed to continue praying, affirming and visualizing myself completing my mission successfully, until it happened. It felt as if God took my hand and said, "Stay close to me. Everything is going to be all right."

When I arrived at work, I noticed a friend had emailed me an article from the DailyOM online magazine about declaring our intentions. This article was entitled, "Declaring Our Intentions," and explained how important it is for us to restate our intentions, when we're feeling stuck and doubtful. It suggested we sit quietly and reaffirm our desires repeatedly, in even more detail, and then trust they would materialize in perfect timing. This enables us to push through the clouds of negative thoughts and realize the good that is in store for us.

Once more, I was reassured that, when self-doubt creeps in, simply restate my desires and continue moving in the direction of my dreams. I was being encouraged to persevere.

The grey clouds of limitation and self-doubt can be pushed aside rather gently, by taking the hand of the One who knows your perfection. The wisdom for living a fully satisfying life already exists *within* you. You don't have to search anywhere outside yourself for the answers. Your higher mind already contains your Truth. Simply reach for the Light within you. Dare to step out of the familiar, into the arms of the Marvelous, and be that truthful, bright, beautiful spirit you were created to be.

Nourishing our minds daily with beautiful, light-filled thoughts aligns us with all that is good and keeps us focused. The following devotionals were designed to support you on your journey into the warm Light. As you read them, consider writing down any ideas or thoughts that come to you. Put into your own words what the statement means to you. Writing down your ideas and goals is a simple, but powerful action, designed to lead you to a more fulfilling life.

Ponder these statements daily for maximal use. There are thirty declarations of truth, designed to shift your consciousness. You can read one statement and focus on it for a day, or choose one and live it for a week or a month and then choose a new one. You will know what works best for you.

May these declarations gently kiss away any idea that keeps you from experiencing your own beautiful light.

Fulfillment

I'm standing in the Breath of God, where all my dreams and desires for good are materialized. God is the Source of all that I am. His Wisdom exists within me, His Strength stands beside me, and His Love is in front of and behind me. His Light permeates my being. Wherever I am, He is also. My greatest desire, He has already fulfilled. The Light of God now dissolves any perceived hurdles that stand between my desires and me.

Solace

I breathe with God today and allow His Breath to calm my fears and direct my steps. I inhale His Beauty, as I look around and give thanks for all that I have and all that I am. His Breath kisses my life with the Light of Love and I am grateful.

I visualize my grand desires, while breathing with God, knowing I am safe and entitled to live a marvelous life.

Transcendence

Every cell in my body was created with Light, by the Light. Love is expressed through my mind, as I join with Spirit in living my life. My daily activities are nothing more than opportunities to express the Perfection that lives within me and to salute the Perfection that lives in everyone and everything. I look out onto the world with the eyes of Love.

Harmony

I see myself living and experiencing the kind of life I have always wanted. I take time each day to be with Spirit and this creates harmony in all my relationships and interactions. My mind is at peace, even in uncertain situations. I know that, come what may, I am always safe. Love surrounds me, because I give Love wherever I am. I am happy. I am healthy. I am free. I am Love.

Manifestation

I am lifted higher today, with each loving thought. My mind is centered on the Light within and thoughts of Beauty, Truth, Love and Success spring forth throughout the day, directing me to a place of wholeness. From this Christ Consciousness, all action is right action. Each spoken word is perfectly choreographed to bring forth the highest and best for all, in every situation. My life is a beautiful manifestation of Light. Everything is working together in perfect harmony, as I breathe in and out with God.

Union

The God Self within me knows only wholeness, fullness, abundance and happiness. This true Nature radiates well-being throughout my body and my life. Today, I become aware of this Nature and trust that it will guide me in all my affairs. I ask that my mind be attuned to this One Self and understand that as I have asked, it has been given me. I give thanks and praise that it is so.

Guidance

Fear no longer grips my life. Whenever fearful thoughts appear, I simply ask Christ for a miracle, a new way of seeing, and my mind is restored to Truth. This one critical step eliminates any perceived roadblocks and I am free to soar. The way is made clear for me to succeed on a grand scale. The door is wide open for me to walk through.

Guidance is given me, whenever requested. I am not alone. The Force of the entire Universe supports me. I am loved. And so it is.

Trust

I stand in Faith, while holding the hand of Christ, and accept happiness as my birthright. The old, dead thoughts of the past are gone. Sparkling, brilliant ideas for my radiant future replace them. I experience a life of self-acceptance and peace. I am capable of accomplishing my dreams, as I trust in Christ for their manifestation. I am willing to relinquish a life of mediocrity, by stepping gracefully into the Marvelous.

Appreciation

Today, I am grateful for all I am and all that I have. I appreciate the beautiful Nature within me and treat others and myself with great kindness. I lovingly care for my spirit, mind and body. I represent love, perfect health and happiness.

Vision

As I look out onto the landscape of my life, I am willing to relinquish all darkness and see the Beauty of God instead, which exists in all people, situations and things. I am willing to notice the Beautiful One, even if only for a moment. For in this holy instance, eternity exists and the beauty in my life and the world is strengthened.

Simplicity

There is a Divine Flow to my life and all life. I am so valued, the Universe lovingly supports me at every turn. The right thought is given to me at the exact moment needed. The appropriate people for the accomplishment of my desires show up, as if on cue, and ideas to raise me higher fill my mind. Simplistic perfection surrounds me and I am grateful.

I step into this Divine Flow through non-resistance and realize life does not have to be a struggle. I accept my life as it is now and embrace its inherent beauty. I acknowledge the Divine within me and trust that I will be given the guidance needed to achieve my grandest dreams. I am deeply loved. I, in turn, love my body, my life and myself and extend this unlimited love to all I meet.

Confidence

I take a moment to be still and to acknowledge that all is well. Regardless of the physical circumstances manifesting in my life, in this holy instance I am holding Christ's hand and I am safe. I pause long enough to feel His presence with me. He leans His Strength into me and I become more confident. I can face whatever the day may bring, because He has prepared the way for me and walks with me. I am never alone. I listen for His guidance throughout the day, as He directs my steps. I am open to receiving His ideas. I am willing to embrace His love.

Honesty

I see myself experiencing a life of complete contentment. I give myself permission to be the beautiful spirit I was created to be. I celebrate my unique gifts, by expressing them in lovely ways. I am courageous and risk revealing myself, honestly and truthfully, to others. As I begin to convey my authentic self, something magnificent occurs. More of what brings me great happiness shows up effortlessly. The synchronicity of life gently replaces the old, rigid life, once rooted in fear. I remain flexible and awake, as I move through this magnificently brilliant life. I have become a true expression of Love. I am content.

Divinity

I was created to live a life of freedom from fear and worry. I am a divine being, with the ability to express my beautiful nature in marvelous ways. Each time I am confronted with a fearful thought or idea, I overcome fear by asking God for a miracle. I am strengthened, each time I refuse to allow fear to limit me. The more frequently I practice this principle, the less threatening fear becomes. I am free to live an unlimited life.

Generosity

I honor the dignity of others and myself with my thoughts, words and actions. When noticing someone suffering or struggling with anger, I send this person kind thoughts. I remember times in my own life when I, too, wanted to be free from suffering. I choose to give this gift freely to others, without expectations. Holding benevolent thoughts of another in my mind naturally aligns me with Spirit. It feels wonderful to increase the beauty in the world. My life is of value. I matter.

Assurance

Today, I stand steady in the Light. I desire the Light. I choose the Light over darkness. I trust that with every situation that arises, I will be given what is the highest and best for all involved. I move through all aspects of my life with calm certainty.

I am guided, ever so gently, down the path that is best for me. I become happier and kinder as I walk with Spirit. My life is elegant.

Release

I make room in my heart for Forgiveness. My heart is big enough, powerful enough, and strong enough to forgive anyone who has caused me distress. I take a moment to be still and invite into my heart anyone who has caused me discomfort, knowing that Spirit will burn away any residue that keeps me negatively connected to this person, in any way. I am safe, as I stand in the Light and allow Spirit to transform this relationship into all it was intended to be. I now release this person, knowing that as I do, a new sense of peace will begin to take hold in my mind. I now move forward in life, with greater strength and wisdom. All is well.

Receptiveness

I have been given the power to live an uncommon life and I am grateful. I embrace the magnificence of my being, which is a reflection of the Divine, and give thanks for my wonderful life.

I desire all the good that is in store for me and I am receptive to receiving it here and now. My life is filled to the brim with happiness.

Clarity

I give birth to a new life today. I relinquish all thoughts about past situations, people, regrets and disappointments or future concerns. I release it all and stand in this virgin moment, ready to create a new future, by simply being completely present now.

Awakening to this holy moment gives me the clarity needed to choose what is the highest and best for all concerned, in any situation. I listen attentively for Spirit's direction and trust the guidance provided.

I am awake and all is well in my world.

Security

Wherever I go, I am safe, because the Light of Love surrounds my every step. It is impossible for me to journey anywhere this Benevolent Force is not and, for that, I am truly grateful. This warm, golden Light embraces, nourishes and comforts me. I relax into my own skin, with a new understanding that all is well. There is nowhere else I need to be, other than right here in this holy moment, at one with Life, at one with Love. I am grateful for this life.

Wisdom

The Beautiful One, who resides within me, is above all my circumstances. This Father, Mother, God is larger than any particular situation I encounter and lovingly grants all Wisdom needed, to successfully manage my life and affairs. I rely on this Wisdom, whenever I am faced with any decision, and trust that I will receive the appropriate answer, in perfect timing. I am in tune with the flow of my life and am willing to listen to the Voice of Spirit. I place my confidence in God.

Tolerance

I give thanks for every person in my life. There is something to learn from each one and I take a moment to relinquish any resistance I may have towards anyone. As I open up to my life in full acceptance, right now, peace abounds and happiness accompanies me. All is well in my life. I am so thankful.

Gratitude

I give thanks in all situations today, regardless of their appearance. In doing so, I unleash the power for right action to take place. Giving thanks awakens my connection with the Divine within and reminds me that the One who knows all things has everything under control and is free to lead. All is well. I am safe.

Abundance

I celebrate all the gifts I have been granted today. I acknowledge the vast display of Beauty in my life, as I move lovingly through my day. I notice the colorful sky, fresh flowers, a friendly smile, a compliment, a kind word, good news, a loving thought and the wonderful sound of a loved one's voice. I spend time in gratitude today, for I have been given so much. I am blessed. Yes, I am blessed indeed.

Liberation

Today, I am willing to think with Spirit, so my mind may be raised to new heights. I relinquish the stories of my past that say I'm not smart enough, rich enough, pretty enough or good enough to live a life of happiness. These are simply ideas, which keep me stuck, and are not the Truth about me.

The Truth is that happiness and love surround me in this very instant. I belong to Love and exist in Love. Love is always available and ready to comfort, guide and support me. This Benevolent Presence, which exists within me, is the Source of all my happiness, security and prosperity. It has been within me all along. I wait no longer for the magnificent gifts in store for me. I say, "Yes," to them all, knowing that I deserve a rich and fulfilling life.

Courage

Each step I take towards the accomplishment of my desires is a step away from fear. I am willing to move through fear and self-doubt, by walking the path of the unknown. As I remain disciplined and continue on my course, fear has less and less power over me. I see myself realizing my deepest desires.

Accomplishment

As I move through life, towards my goal, all doors open easily for me. The illusion of struggle has evaporated and I step forward, with great momentum, to accomplish my goals. I am on the road to success and it feels wonderful. I see myself confidently realizing my desires, laughing and having great fun.

My life has become a delightful manifestation of success, as *I define it.*

Prosperity

I marvel at the abundance of opportunities for me to experience real joy in my life. I am surrounded by prospects of good fortune, because I am one with Spirit. Wherever I go, my good follows. It is not something I have to grasp for or cling to, for it is always readily available to me. I allow things to move gently into and out of my life, with complete acceptance, knowing I am always fulfilled, because I am an unlimited spiritual being.

Vocation

Love uses my hands today to express Itself. The work that I do in the world is cultivated with Love, making it a Divine Expression. I am keenly attentive to the details of my life, allowing me to fully enjoy the process. I contemplate all the good I've received, from the work of my loving hands, and I am grateful. I live this day with an open heart and mind, ready to freely give and receive love wherever I go.

Contentment

There is nothing to fear, for the Light has already been granted. I am willing to brush aside any thoughts of self-doubt, lack or limitation, by saying, "Yes," to the Light within me. As I take the first step in reaching for the Light, I will be given a new vision of myself, which raises me higher on my journey towards happiness and contentment. This day, I experience the joy of living the life of freedom I deserve.

*A few simple prayers designed to lighten your mind
and lift your spirit.*

A Celebration of Light

I celebrate Your Light today, God, and give thanks that it is always readily available in unlimited supply. I stretch out my soul's arms and lovingly welcome You. I harness Your Light today and freely extend it outward into the world, allowing it to bless others in perfect ways. Your Golden Light is powerful enough to bring healing to a hurting, fearful world, and I am so grateful.

Honoring the Infinite One

It is enough that I have You by my side, Infinite One. I am in need of nothing else. My appreciation for Your Presence in my life, and Your Devotion to me, is too large for words to hold. May my actions today serve as a means of honoring You, in all aspects of my life. May I be a blessing onto the world.

Owning Our Light

Teach me how to recognize Your Light in others, Beautiful One. Train my mind to be alert to Your Guidance. Lean Your Strength into me, so I may be the person You created me to be: happy, free, unlimited, grace-filled and successful.

Today, may I own the Light that I am.

Dripping with Gratitude

Here I stand, in this elegant moment, dripping with gratitude for all I am, all I have, and this life so beautiful.

Dearest Friend, teach me how to carry myself in a manner that honors all of life. May my actions be consistent with Your will for me.

If, at some point, I lose sight of this blessed gift, Dearest Friend, gently remind me of its value.

Divinely Uplifted

Lord, raise my mind to new heights, so I may learn how to think with You. Draw me close today and hold me in such a way that I know all is well. Sprinkle my mind with Your radiant Light, so I can remember our connection and how powerfully beautiful it is. Let me experience Your invisible hands lifting me higher, Lord.

From this holy space, I simply love You.

The Gift of Grace

May I experience grace this day, Beloved. The kind of grace that penetrates every cell of my body, radiating outward, until it touches the Light in others. Tickle my soul with Your warm Light, Golden One. Help me to experience my true Nature, which is rooted deeply in contentment.

Awaken my spirit with Your smile, and gently remove any thoughts that keep me from experiencing the joy of You.

Bountiful Blessings

I ask for a blessing on anyone who is feeling burdened for any reason, Dearest Friend. They may be experiencing financial pressures, relationship disappointments, health concerns, loss of a loved one or loneliness. Pour Your Strength into them, Beloved. Kiss their lives with the Light of Love. Lift them gently into the arms of Grace.

Send a host of angels to guide their steps and calm their minds. Hold them in such a way that they understand You are near. May they experience Your Presence this day.

A Beacon of Light

Beloved Friend, Your radiant light beckons me once again and, this time, I walk towards it. Please keep me from stumbling around in darkness on my way to You, Gentle One. Make clear my path. Guide me through the fearful shadows, so I may see all darkness as simply an illusion. Remind me that Your Light overpowers all darkness and I am safe.

Immersed in Love's Light

I stand in the Light of Love and call on Your holy name. I need You, God. Renew my mind with Your grace-filled thoughts. Breathe new life into me, that I may begin again and choose a path higher than yesterday. It is my destiny to rise to new heights. Please show me how.

May Your thoughts, which fill my mind, direct all my actions. All is well.

Extending Grace

Lean the Light of Forgiveness unto our world, Beloved. Let it shimmer with such brilliance, that we can't help but see it, embrace it and extend it to others. My heart is opened wide to receive all the love You are sending. I allow it to flow through me, touching others, as I greet them throughout the day.

I hold the thought of Love in my mind and realize this simple act of Grace changes my world.

BE BEAUTY

INTRODUCTION

A new expression is evolving. It is one of great strength and beauty. Powerful spiritual ideas now caress the hearts and minds of people all over the world, exposing and celebrating the magnificent spirit within. This is our moment.

It appears the task given this generation is to muster enough spiritual stamina to stand amidst the fearful images flickering in our world today and claim a higher order for ourselves.

As we pull our gaze away from fear-based images and place our attention on the Spirit of Love within, we own our greatness. The old belief structure, once dominated by fear, can now be dissolved and replaced with the Light of Love, if we so choose.

Perhaps it is time to pause, collect our senses and choose a different route. It's easy to feel powerless, when observing worldly events, which seem beyond our control. However, power comes from choice and deciding how we live the moments of our lives, regardless of our life situations.

If we want to build spiritual muscles, we must represent Love, while in the midst of fear. There are countless ways we can accomplish this. Love's light can be summoned from behind fear's veil of darkness, anywhere, anytime, and with anyone.

We can increase the Light in our lives through our interactions with people, the way we decorate our home or office, the thoughts we hold about ourselves and others and the words we choose to speak. We can decide to be generous with our time, money or talents, even in the face of apparent scarcity. I have found nothing turns the illusion of insufficiency into abundance quicker than an attitude of gracious giving and gratefulness.

I have practiced a variety of methods to expand the Love in all facets of my life and discovered a select few, which magnified the beauty in my life so intensely, and so fully, that I wanted to share them with others. It is my intention that the following ideas decorate your life with an amount of loveliness so grand, you find yourself kneeling at the feet of Grace.

Say Hello to Love

One of the easiest ways to draw the Spirit of Love into our lives is to recognize Her, as She flirts with us throughout the day. The force of Love is everywhere, dancing all around us in great delight, just waiting for us to notice Her. When there is a long line of traffic and someone stops to let you in, Love is waving, "hello." When you have trouble finding something in a store and someone offers to help you, Love is saying, "I will show you where it is, dear." When you are experiencing a troublesome day and someone offers you a kind word, Love is saying, "It's okay, I am here for you."

Love is constantly speaking to us, encouraging us to continue moving forward on our journey. As we begin to listen, we will see Love everywhere and in everyone. She will show up in the most unexplained places and in ways that unquestionably point to Her. It is as if She is winking and saying, "Hi, it's me!" Love wants you to discover, embrace and join Her. Your slightest invitation will draw Her near to you. The more steps you take towards Love, the more you will find Her eagerly greeting and encouraging you at every turn.

Love smiled at me in the form of the garbage man one day. While walking my spirited Jack Russell Terrier, Bailey, I saw the garbage man working diligently to quickly collect and empty all the cans of garbage on the street. Gratitude filled me, as I realized how much his work benefited me and considered what a hassle it would be, if I had to haul my garbage to the dump weekly. I smiled and sent him a silent, "Thank you."

He smiled wide and bright and continued about his business. A few moments later, I caught up with him again and he shouted, "You look like a ray of sunshine. God bless you!"

What a perfect testament to the Love inside me, bowing to the Love within him, and the Love contained in him saluting the Love that exists in me. When we are willing to see the force of Love in another, it is that Love which is reflected back to us with grace and gratitude.

Sending silent blessings to others is such a powerful practice. People often respond to these silent messages in the most miraculous ways. Their reply or looks of gratitude, shinning in their eyes, decorate my life in the most delightful manner. Life then moves with merriment, as the beauty in the world is enlarged.

Give Thanks

Have you ever noticed how giving thanks for someone or something in your life generates more gratitude? It's as if thoughts of thanksgiving piggyback each other. This was certainly the case one warm summer afternoon, when I arrived home from work to find my air conditioner didn't work. My wonderful husband, Mike, greeted me in the garage, as I stepped out of my car, to inform me that our air conditioner had died. Suddenly, the Bible verse, 1 Thessalonians 5:18, came to mind. "In everything, give thanks." I paused briefly, said a silent, "Thank you," then listened as Mike explained the situation.

When he finished speaking, I calmly replied, "Ok, it sounds like we need a new system." I could see the concerned look on his face, as we both knew this was an unplanned expense. Again, the message, "In all things, give thanks," came to mind. Once more, I gave a silent "Thank you" for this situation at hand and for God's perfect timing.

Almost immediately, I felt deeply peaceful. My mind began to recall one past event after another, where God had provided for my family, and I realized He would meet our needs in this situation as well. I reassured Mike that all would be well, as we took the necessary steps to replace our air conditioner.

While unloading the groceries from the car, I became grateful for the continuous rainfall and recognized it as a real blessing. It kept our house much cooler, because we could open the doors and windows. As it turned out, this was the only day all week with so much rain! I watched my husband, as he worked to rectify the situation, and swelled with appreciation for him, for all the good he brings our family and for his keen mechanical knowledge!

While preparing dinner, I felt thankful for the healthy food we had to eat. Before long, I caught myself humming and feeling especially fortunate for my good life. Gratitude had indeed delivered me into the arms of Grace and lifted me above my current life situation to a place of gladness.

Love the Life You Are In

Sometimes, it seems more comfortable to rest beneath the branch of darkness than to claim our spot in the sunlight. It somehow feels more natural. However, when the gravity of darkness becomes intense enough, we begin to realize that it really is not a cozy place after all, just a more familiar one.

Right now, in this moment, we have everything needed to rise above our current life situations and experience peace. We have the ability to observe our thoughts and select the ones that bring more Beauty into our lives. This is such an important gift, because most unhappiness in life is a result of our thinking, not external conditions or another person. Our mind constantly evaluates people and situations, categorizing them as desirable or undesirable. Events that don't meet our anticipated outcome we typically label, "unfavorable," which leaves us feeling discouraged and dissatisfied.

To turn the landscape of our mind into a beautiful garden of healthy ideas, we must tend to it regularly, with patience, wisdom and loving care. We need to remove old, dead thoughts and beliefs, which no longer serve us, and replace them with lovely new ideas. Many avenues exist to support us in achieving a new mind pattern. One that works consistently well for me is the following two-step process.

Step One

Become aware of the thoughts marching across your mind. What are they telling you? Are they thoughts of lack, fear, limitation, doom and gloom or self-doubt? You can usually recognize which thoughts are commanding your attention by observing your mood. If you're feeling anxious, stressed, fearful or worried, chances are you're listening to fear-based, critical or judgmental ideas.

Step Two

Once you unveil the dark thoughts, they require releasing. I normally need help with this step and ask the Holy Spirit for a miracle, a new way of seeing the situation or person. I then pause briefly and imagine myself handing the problematic event or person over to Jesus for healing. Lesson 213 in *A Course in Miracles* states,

"All things are lessons God would have me learn. A lesson is a miracle which God offers to me, in place of thoughts I made that hurt me. What I learn from Him instead becomes the way I am set free. And so I choose to learn His lessons and forget my own."

This simple two-step process never fails to return my mind to a state of peace. It releases me from fear's clutches and places me in the arms of Grace, where I belong. As we continue to release and forgive our life experiences, we become more flexible and less resistant to life. Then, life can work for us and bloom into magnificent manifestations. Now, we are free to love the people in our lives, the work at hand and the process of this benevolent life.

Practice Forgiveness

If there are people in your life you are not in harmony with, consider spending a few moments seeing them surrounded by gorgeous white light. You can do this while stuck in traffic, sitting at a red light or on the phone with them.

Simply close your eyes and picture them, bathed in brilliant white light. Observe the light, as it grows stronger and brighter, until they become one with it. Witness the luminous rays expanding in strength, until your entire mind radiates.

Do this daily, or each time you think of them or see them, and watch with gladness, as the relationship is transformed. I have found, when practicing this principle regularly, the people I surrounded by light moved gently out of my life or the relationship became a satisfying inter-action. Seeing one surrounded by light releases them from judgment. As we free others from our judgments, we free ourselves.

Speak Beauty Filled Words

Each day, for forty days, let the first words you speak to your spouse, partner, children, friend or co-worker be something kind or loving. Focus on what is positive in them and in your life. Find the Greatness within them and speak to that loveliness. Consider how their presence in your life benefits you.

Sometimes, it may feel as if our mind is programmed to see first what is not right in another person. However, the mind will concentrate on whatever directive we provide. All that is really needed to develop a new thought process is a willingness and intent to see the Exquisite in someone else.

Everyone has something worth appreciating. It may take an extra minute or two to discover, but it is there, waiting to be unveiled. Nourishing someone's mind with healthy ideas is powerful. It creates an opening for one to awaken to a higher vision of himself.

Acknowledging the Greatness in others benefits us, too. As we focus our attention on the Light in others, our own Light is magnified and the Beauty in the world is enlarged.

Every interaction then becomes an opportunity to welcome the Magnificent into our lives and to embrace it with warm affection. The majesty needed to change this old world exists within you. Let us welcome the Light together and allow Beauty to engulf the world.

Choose the unseen possibilities, which are above the images of this physical world. Greatness arrives at the slightest invitation, because Love is always greater than fear. Dare to choose Love.

Give the Gift of Listening

People are starving to be heard and listening to someone, with complete attention, can have amazing healing results. Real listening can shift relationships from discord to harmony, help us to connect with others and strengthen our self-concept.

This is an easy principle to practice, because it can be done anywhere, anytime, with anyone. Simply select someone in your life, who could benefit from your undivided attention. It can be a spouse, neighbor, friend, co-worker or the cashier at the grocery store.

When this person is ready to talk, listen with your entire being. Speak very little. Quiet your mind, by placing your full attention on what he or she is saying. Continually bring your attention back to the person speaking, if your mind begins to wander. One trick I use to keep my mind from roaming, while someone is talking with me, is to say silently, "Peace be with you." This statement places my attention back on the person speaking, instead of me.

The person you are listening to will most likely leave your presence with a sense of fulfillment, knowing he or she was heard, and you will have given of yourself in a meaningful way. You may find, with much delight, that people in your life begin listening more attentively to you, as you apply this concept consistently, for indeed, as we give, so do we receive.

Observe Nature

Enlarging the Beauty in our lives is easy to achieve, because there is so much natural loveliness around us. We only have to place our attention on it, in order for the Beauty in our lives to grow.

Listen to the birds sing, while walking to your car in the parking lot. Watch ducks glide across a pond or observe how the butterfly dances along the flower tops. Notice the sunrise, on your drive into work, and watch how the sky smiles or witness the sun's surrender to the moon and feel the love in your heart expand.

Observing nature can help us connect with the gentleness and perfection that exists in our lives at this moment. It requires little time, yet generates significant peace. Opening our minds to the Divine in nature honors the richness of our lives and relaxes the cycle of frenetic thinking, which usually consumes our minds.

SEE BEAUTY

INTRODUCTION

The following poems represent special moments in time, when I saw a beautiful sky, felt a Divine Presence or experienced Love's hand gently touching my heart. Creating them has brought me immense joy and a deeper connection to all that is good in the world. It is my hope they will serve as treasures, sent out into the world, to lighten as many hearts and minds as possible.

I trust these poems will open the window of your heart and mind, so everything lovely can rush towards you, like great ocean waves. May the gifts of love surround you and multiply in all areas of your life.

Invisible Grace

Beloved, all day long
I thank You.

All day long,
I reach for Your hand.

All day long,
You steady me.

You are beautiful,
all day long.

Yellow Flower

Oh, Beautiful One,
You wave Your
smile at me.

I didn't see You earlier,
in that yellow flower
beneath the tree.

I later caught You flirting,
as Your Light danced across
the sea.

Tickle me some more,
my Lord,
until I cannot

BREATHE!

Eternal Moment

Love's treasures sparkle around me,
like fireflies
flickering in the night.

Each dazzling gift captivates
my gaze, as Love replaces
my fright.

My mind is hypnotized with
loveliness,
whether glancing
left, center or right.

Beauty and Truth
now accompany me,
sprinkling my path with
Light.

Kissing Hearts

We live in a universe where
all hearts embrace upon meeting
and chat happily, like old
friends.

How long before we
allow them to
kiss?

My Beloved Winks at Me

Sun-soaked clouds hover together in the
sky's East corner,

setting the stage for
dawn's grand arrival.

Pools of liquid light crown
the pastel clouds,
as the sun's face is slowly unveiled.

Then, as if by magic, it happens:

the sky smiles

and You wink at me.

Believe

The sun peeked around the lazy cloud,
strolling across the
sky.

Adorning trees with majestic light,
only to catch my
eye.

Luminous pearls scattered about,
as far as I could
see.

Beauty lifted me into Her arms
and whispered,

"BELIEVE."

Safe Haven

When the world becomes too heavy,
I close my eyes and rest
my head on my
Beloved's
chest.

And sometimes,
even now,

I am surprised to
awake and find

Her lips pressed
gently against my
forehead.

Beloved Friends

"I love You, it's true," I cried out to the
One Who beats my heart
and counts my
breaths.

Apart from Him,
I do not exist.

He is the ocean
in which my body swims,

the manna that nourishes me,
and every happy thought,
cradled in my mind.

I must go now.

The Golden One
is flirting again

and all my cells

are smiling!

A Love Forgotten

Sometimes I miss You,
when I'm asleep
in the dark

and I have forgotten the touch
of Your hand, curled
softly 'round my
heart.

If only I could remember
what You taught me
at the start,

You and I can never be
separate or
apart.

Magnitude

Look Whose hand

I'm holding.

Now, anything

is

possible.

Breathing with God

Beautiful angel,
standing there soaked in sacredness,
waiting to be liberated from all
that makes you tired,

breathe
in and out with
God.

His invisible hands will
paint smiles on every
cell of your
body,

tickling you with

H
A
P
P
I
N
E
S
S.

Fearless

When you have gone as far as you
think you can,

expand the borders.

When you are feeling lonely
or afraid,

expand the borders.

When you feel that life has
let you down,

expand the borders
of your mind,

by walking the path you
fear you can't.

Love's Invitation

The sun gently nudges the
sleeping sky awake

and the soft, petal pink sky yawns with
immaculate beauty.

In purity and perfection, a
new day is born,

bursting with opportunities

to cuddle

the Beautiful One.

A Regal Affair

Nature bows in penetrating silence,
as the sun kisses the
virgin snow.

No horns, trumpets or drums
are necessary to celebrate
this regal affair.

The Gentle One appears in
the hush of the still morning
air

and lovingly watches me

adoring

Him.

Pregnant Moon

I lost myself in the
gracious light of the pregnant moon.

Casting all pretension aside left me cheek to cheek,
hand in hand, with the
Beautiful One.

Together Let's Sing

One gentle autumn afternoon,
when idleness had emptied me,

I watched palm trees sway in the sky's arms,
while the wind chased glittering sun drops across the pond

and my heart's window blew open,
releasing happy songs for all to
sing.

Love's Reflection

Drink in Love's elixir,

beautiful angel,

then hold a mirror close,
to glimpse dazzling moonbeams
streaming from

your holy

F
A
C
E.

A Sacred Opening

I yield to Love, in
this space emptied of words
and cumbersome ideas,

where a thousand pores
sing halleluiah,

while happiness and all
its relatives dance wildly
across my heart,

drunk with gratitude

for a delicious glimpse
of the Divine.

An Ocean of Happiness

Once, when my heart felt sad,
I cried out to the
Gentle One

and waves of love
splashed against my heart,

sowing seeds of happiness

that blossomed, when
sprinkled with the light of the
moon.

Divine Comfort

Oh, Beautiful One,
lead me to the Light, where my
heart camps for free

and my soul is drenched in holiness,

while my mind covets
Thee.

Freedom

When my belly is full,
I feel rich.

When my mind is clear,
I feel invincible.

When my heart kisses Yours,
Beloved,

I am free.

Certainty

My Beloved's face is
always turned
towards
me.

His quiet Light
and endearing look
are fixed upon me,

revealing my heritage
and establishing my worth.

One glance in His direction and
He rushes in to greet me,
throwing Himself in front of me.

One glance.

Eternally United

No space exists
between my Beloved
and me.

No breath is unshared.

There is no gap to
explore and fill with
nothingness.

Not even a flicker of light
from the brightest flame
could wedge a place
between us.

We are eternally united in
one loving gaze,

laughing hysterically at the
idea we could ever be anything
less.

A Channel for Grace

Flashes of glittering light
massage my mind,

as I think of You,
Beautiful One.

Each alluring stroke wiggles me awake,
to witness Beauty being
born.

This world is now so beautiful,
when seen through the eyes of Grace.

No fear is possible.

Love fills every
space.

Sky Miracles

A deck of clouds, swollen
with the sun's sweat,
emblazons the sleepy sky,

commanding my attention
with its immense,
unrefined beauty,

brilliant enough to extinguish
any cherished thought
not born of

LOVE.

A Holy Connection

Who is the silent witness
housed within me,
rooted in certainty,

linking me to eternity with
a sacred, unbreakable bond

and uniting me with all that is
marvelous in

one holy Breath?

Soulful Experience

My soul is like a leaf, resting atop
a tranquil river, on a
lazy summer afternoon,

content to glide peacefully along
the water, while gazing into
heaven's face,

unconcerned with the direction
the current will take me,

certain I will arrive at my precise
destination.

Securely Embraced

Fear must be blind.
It continues to woo me.

Can't it see I'm content,
wrapped in the arms of the

Magnificent One?

A Revealing Glimpse

Lift the skirt of your mind
and reveal your Truth.

Your Truth is far more interesting than
the tattered hand-me-down
which conceals it.

Exposed

Our minds are clad
with heaven's
gold.

A treasure we could claim
directly, if we would
dare to disrobe
our

F
E
A
R.

A Return to Love

Flicker Your Light again,
my Beloved,

and I will surely
come.

Oh, how Your beauty
teases me

and into Your arms
I run.

Why Fret?

Would we ever fret again, if
we understood that the

Infinite One is so close,

our lose hair falls directly onto

Her
shoulders?

An Oasis of Grace

All thoughts slumber in this holy moment of release.

Truth has seized self-doubt, liberated me from
the littleness of this world,
and delivered me to a
soothing oasis of grace.

Here in this Sea of Consciousness,
where the borders
of separation dissolve,

Love's appeal is
irresistible.

Sacred Breath

Your holy Breath blows
across my mind, gently removing
all debris,

exposing every sacred thought
for all eternity.

Pregnant blessings abound,
in the wake of Your
warm breeze,

dusting my mind with love and
shrouding it with purity.

Singular

Beloved,

all I need is

You.

A Taste of Bliss

Happiness spills from my mind,
tumbling onto my tongue,

eagerly awaiting an invitation to
irrigate your mind with the

sublime.

Welcomed Visitor

Like the gentle morning fog,
my Beloved arrived unannounced

and quietly smothered my
raging fear with
Love.

THANKS TO...

I am grateful to so many, for their important role in the creation of this book.

Deepest thanks and appreciation go to my Benevolent Friend for the ideas, words, support, love and guidance needed to create this book.

Thanks to my wonderful husband, Mike. His cheerful nature and infinite patience make my heart sing.

Thanks to Dehryl Mason, who embraced this dream with me and provided the encouragement needed for me to step out onto the skinny branches.

Thanks to Donella Vitale, for her friendship, and for cheering me on in the early stages, before I knew what I was doing.

Thanks to Debbie Simpkins, for believing in me and for her innovative distribution ideas.

Thanks to Leah Lindsey, who always sees the highest and best in me.

Thanks to my mother, Jane Mason, for demonstrating persistence.

Thanks to my grandmother, Nell Ison, for nurturing my love of nature.

Thanks to Lin Rhodes, for teaching me how to say, "Yes," to my dreams and myself.

Notes

Friends of Peace Pilgrim. 2003. *Peace Pilgrim: Her Life and Works in Her Own Words.* Santa Fe, New Mexico, http://www.peacepilgrim.org/book/ppbook.pdf.

DailyOM, "Declaring Our Intentions," http://www.today@dailyom.com, (DailyOM), January 10, 2008.

Foundation for Inner Peace. 1996. *A Course In Miracles,* second edition, New York: New York, 394.

About the Author

Breathing with God evolved out of Stacy Isabelle's burning desire to increase the beauty in the world. She believes that anytime we choose to see love in our life situations, instead of fear, we own our Greatness, and the world is transformed in that moment.

One of the top things she intends to do in life is to inspire others to see the divine within themselves and within the world. She has devoted over twenty years to spiritual studies and practices, and has a background in marketing and public relations. Stacy resides in St. Cloud, Florida, where she lives and amazingly beautiful life with her family.

www.ingramcontent.com/pod-product-compliance
Lightning Source LLC
Chambersburg PA
CBHW060804050426
42449CB00008B/1533